# Battling with the Lord

## Journey in the Mind, Body, and Spirit

## Madiline M. Belle

# Dedication

To God be the glory! I thank God for everything He has done to and in me. I dedicate this book to my mother Bernice Stevenson who is a woman of God and God's first gift to me. Thank you for never giving up on me and pushing me to become a woman of God and integrity. Nancy Kingwood a woman of God. I'm thankful for all of the times you encouraged me and the many times you spent praying for me and my family. You were called by God and had been placed in my life for many reasons. I thank you for believing in me when I didn't believe in myself. I thank you for reminding me that Jesus knows my address. Most of all I thank you for your obedience to God when He told you to speak with me.

I want to thank my children Tre'von Woods, Marvin Fields Jr., Jada Fields and my special friend Rodney Sparks for supporting me always and for accepting me and knowing the will of God comes first in spite of your needs. Thank you Evion Matthews you have been my dad and I'm thankful and grateful for everything you have done for me but most of the love you give to me. Thank you to my sister Janisha Davidson for your unconditional love for me; you are your sister's keeper. Thank you to my friend Erika Johnson for being a friend at all times; I'm truly blessed to have you in my life. Thank you my brother Idelin Augustin you are the first man of God I have had in my life. Thank you for having faith in me and for all of your uplifting and encouraging words. You are a living witness of my journey! Thank you to my brothers Robert and Kendall Stevenson for always having my back. Thank you to all of the many other people that God has put in my life here on earth. I love and appreciate you all.

## Purpose of this book

This book is about my journey with God. The purpose of this book is to strengthen, motivate, and inspire one to get themselves through some of the most difficult times when walking and building a relationship with God.

We are all made of three things which is mind, body and spirit. Your mind and body are real but it's temporary. It will stay for some time, but it will dissolve over time. I believe we are a spirit in a body walking through this world. Your spirit /soul which is unseen shall live on.

My name is Madiline Belle I was born to Bernice Belle and Robert Stevenson on April 8, 1979 which was also Palm Sunday that year. I 'm a Black American woman from the United States of America. I'm the first born child to both of my parent's one of four children to my mother and eight to my father. I was born and raised in Bridgeport, Connecticut. I'm a mother of three wonderful children Tre'von Woods, Marvin Fields Jr., and Jada Fields. Most of all I'm a child of God and I'm a part of the body of Christ.

# To God be the Glory!

All glory belongs to God! People tend to believe they are the reason for everything they have become and for the things they have when in fact it is God. God is the only one in control of the universe. Everything that is on earth and in heaven belongs to Him. Glory to God for everything we can see, touch, feel, smell, hear, taste, imagine, and even the unimaginable things that IIe only knows. Each day you are given the gift of life to glorify God in many ways. You can tell Him through prayer, praise and worship, witness to someone about Him, do something to help someone else, love people unconditionally, serve others, make Him known of all nations, most of all live your life in the reflection of God because you are living proof of God. Remember to give credit when it's do so glorify God in everything you do!

Therefore, whether you eat or drink, or whatever you do, do all to the glory of God. 1 Corinthians 10:31 New King James Version (NKJV)

# Spread love

You should love God just for who He is and not for what He does for you .We could never make the sacrifice that God has done for us by sacrificing His one and only begotten son, so we could have eternal life. I don't know anyone that is willing to give up their child so others can live. There are so many negative things in the world such as people spread lies, rumors, hate, racism, violence, jealousy, and envy. At one point I had decided to stay off social media for over a year due to all the negative things that were posted. As I knew many of the people who were posting, it bothered me to know what was being put out into the world. I believe we speak what's in our hearts. I realized that change starts with yourself, so I decided no more negativity would I tolerate and it didn't matter who posted, liked or commented. You have to take a stand for what you believe in even when others don't agree. God wants you to be positive by spreading His light into this world by love, peace, joy, respect, hope, comfort, and blessings to others.

For God so loved the world that He gave His only begotten Son, that whoever believes in Him should not perish but have everlasting life. John 3:16 New King James Version (NKJV)

Those who accept my commandments and obey them are the ones who love me. And because they love me, my Father will love them. And I will love them and reveal myself to each of them." John 14:21 New Living Translation (NLT)

# Relationship with God

Having a relationship with God is really important in reality it is the most important relationship you will ever have. The best way to build a relationship with God is by reading the Holy Bible. I remain thirsty and wanting to know about God each day. You must spend time with God and know His word. Going to church and receiving the word from your disciple is great, but you will only get their perception on what they read, so you must also establish a relationship for yourself. I used to watch televised Christian leaders on Sunday mornings instead of going to church. I also used to listen gospel music at home and in my car which then I believed that was enough for God. In fact what I was doing was clearly not what God desires from us. He wants more than Sunday visits in and out of the sanctuary what I was doing was satisfying myself and not God. If you think about it we put time into our relationships with our spouse, family, children, friends, and coworkers. God wants the same kind of relationship, He wants your time and besides there is so much knowledge to receive from Him. Nothing or no one should come before God. He is a jealous God and wants to be put first. Set time aside for God because He is that important. You should talk about God like you do your love ones. God should be magnified at all times after all He has blessed you with other people in your life. You may want to find out why He has done that. As I stated previously building an intimate relationship with God means spending intimate time with Him reading the Bible, prayer, meditating on Him and His words daily. Spending time with God and in the word of God is where you get your faith. God's word is true and in order to have faith you must know the word for yourself.

So then faith comes by hearing, and hearing by the word of God. Romans 10:17 New King James Version (NKJV)

# Who is your friend?

Many people will claim to be your friend but are they really your friend? I realized I had people that claimed to be my friend until I started getting closer to God. Many people claim to be your friend and lead you to clubs, bars, sex, drugs, violence, crime, gossip, gangs, and drama. A friend who really cares about you we lead you to God. A true friend wants the best for you at all times and wants to see you joyful and building a relationship with God. I have family and friends that will travel in and out of the state and country with me but won't travel across town to worship with me. You may have to evaluate your relationships with people and know what role you really are in .Those who love you will want you to have a relationship with the best friend one can have. You should want to be around people who want to encourage you to live righteous just like God. Trust in knowing that you will have times in your life that will require support from others. God has put people in places to help you in your growth with a relationship with Him, the good, and the trials that you will have to face in life. You can always ask God to lead you to the right person and or place. If you're going to be led by anyone let it God.

## Role changes people change

There are times when people around you show there true selves. I had received a promotion at work which revealed who was a friend and who was a foe. Before the promotion we consider ourselves friends as well as coworkers. The day my supervisor stated I would be promoted I noticed the shift in people's body language. Everyone said " congratulations " however I could tell it wasn't real due to the fact that I knew them for some time and the nonverbal things such as looking at one another, the facial expressions as if one wanted to say ,what's going on? Why her? It should have been me! I was even told I didn't qualify because of my lack of education for the position. I was embraced by some of my friends who accepted the promotion I received genuine congratulations and even a card. I was also shown congratulations by the reluctance I received from those when having to perform task when I was the one who had to assign it to them. I was called names such as a gopher and a snitch, I was told reasons why they thought I got the positions but, I held my head up high and continued to do my job in spite of how others had perceived me. Your true friends will respect you at all times money, positions, and power should affect a real friendship. I had stepped out and tried something different with another company and which I could engage with family members and friends. I remember a relative bringing a friend over for the presentation. The friend of my relative was interested and wanted to join unfortunately my relative revealed a side of herself I hadn't seen. My relative convinced her friend not to join as she listened to my goals with the company. Some people are comfortable seeing you where you are now and they will not be comfortable were you want to go or where God is taking you .Many people hide behind a mask of deception and their mask sometimes isn't revealed until something happens. With growth relationships will change amongst people in your life, some will be happy and some will be jealous and envious. There are also many people in my life that were loving and were only there for a short period of time.

God will place people in your life to get you through some tough times. Some have moved or time has separated us physically but I'm forever grateful for the time we shared. No matter what happens keep moving forward, beware of who is for you and who is against you and forgive them who do you wrong. Every relationship will play a role either for a season, blessing and some will be a life lesson learned.

A sound heart is life to the body, but envy is rottenness to the bones. Proverbs 14:30  New King James Version (NKJV)

Therefore, whatever you want men to do to you, do also to them, for this is the Law and the Prophets. Matthew 7:12 New King James Version (NKJV)

# From the circle to the cross /Body of Christ

When you build a relationship with God your circle will change. Before I surrendered all to Jesus I had many people who I considered to be great friends and family. As I got closer to God I realized some of my relationships were changing. I had people that I used to hang with, danced in clubs and at home with, consumed alcohol, and smoked marijuana with that no longer wanted to be in my company. The process isn't always easy, but it is worth it. Every time God closes one door He opens another. I found out when you have a true friend they will pray and lead you in the right direction. I lost some people, but I gained many more friends in Christ. I found out they like to dance, have gatherings, and unite even more than the company I had lost. There is no alcohol or drugs involved but a supernatural high is better than any temporary one I had before Christ. You may have to give up being around some people who want to keep you in a worldly environment, it may be even someone as close to you as a family member. I promise you the love of God is much better.

# Pray for your enemies

During one summer I had a neighbor who betrayed me by smiling in my face and then stabbing me in my back. She decided she would talk about me to another neighbor and I wouldn't find out, but I did. My first thought was to confront her, but instead I prayed for her. During the winter months she would then ask to borrow my shovel and each time I said yes.

Sometimes you may have someone around you that may befriend you but you must pray for them. Forgiveness is what we all should be doing and also praying for those who do you wrong.

"You have heard that it was said, 'You shall love your neighbor and hate your enemy.' But I say to you, love your enemies, bless those who curse you, do good to those who hate you, and pray for those who spitefully use you and persecute you, that you may be sons of your Father in heaven; for He makes His sun rise on the evil and on the good, and sends rain on the just and on the unjust.

Matthew 5:43-45 New King James Version (NKJV)

# Conflict Religion

Religion can sometimes break families apart no matter how close the relationship is. My paternal great grandmother and grandmother were both Jehovah Witness'. I know who they are, but we have never been able to establish a long term relationship due to religion. My mom has always believed and accepts Jesus as her Lord and Savior. My paternal grandmother has tried to pursue my mom to convert which made her stay away from her. This also caused me to be away because I was a minor child. I remember having birthday's which they wouldn't verbalize the day, but give me funds due to love. It took years for me to tell my grandmother I was disappointed in her because I felt even though I was a child she was still an adult who lived blocks away from me for many years, but never attempted to see me. There were times I would see her for a brief time which we would communicate but not for too long, our relationship always seems to fade fast. She has been supportive to me during the time my daughter was neglected and I'm grateful God had placed her in my life at that time. I have also like my maternal family have accepted Jesus as my Lord and Savior, so when she talks about being a Jehovah Witness I get turned off but I respect her. I love my grandmother and wish we could have a relationship especially knowing she is aging, but God has yet to make that happen. I have accepted that I may never have the bond that I have hoped for because it isn't in the will of God. Although you may not share the same religion or beliefs with someone you can still love and respect them.

# Praying

## Prayer

Communication is a must and praying is an important factor in your relationship with God. We spend time communicating and talking with people all the time. Many times we can forget and neglect to communicate with God. You should talk to Him before talking to anyone else He is the one who is above all. As soon as I awake and my feet hit the floor I kneel and bow down to pray. Prayer should be done every day as many times as possible and needed. I believe that if you do it each day it will become something you can't live without doing. People pray at different times, but I recommend when you wake up, before you go to sleep, before each meal you, before communion you should spend time with God. Some people pray before special events and ceremonies with friends and family, while others pray before tests, before giving a public speech or appearance, games, before receiving news or in a crisis. Praying should begin with meditation. Which is quiet time and I usually listen to music, silence, or on my knees before God. First, one should thank God for everything His love, mercy, grace, protection, compassion, kindness, strength, food, shelter, family, friends and allowing me to be in His presence. Most of all I thank God for just for being who He is. Secondly, one must acknowledge God and magnify His name as most high because He is above everyone and everything. God has all authority on earth and in heaven and He is still on the throne. Thirdly, one must repent and ask for forgiveness. Know that everyone falls short of the glory of God each day and we should all ask God to forgive us for our sins daily. No one is perfect but God which is the reason we will always need Him. Next, one must put in their request of what they are seeking from God. I always ask God to cover me, my family, friends, leaders, and all children of God that are here around the world and on earth in the precious blood of Jesus. You should always ask God what He wants for you to do. Ask Him to lead you in the right direction and to direct your paths.

I always ask God to guide me to the right place, person, or thing. The fifth thing is to thank God for answering your prayer in advance and you must believe by faith it will happen. The last thing you want to do is ask in divine authority which is in the name of Jesus; and always end in agreement by saying Amen. . Communication is a two way process. When you ask someone a question you are expecting an answer back and it's the same thing with God. Sometimes we pray and proceed to the next thing we have to do on our agenda or we pray and God will answer us, but were not listening to Him. Be sure to have some time to listen to God He may have something to tell you.

There may be times when you pray a short prayer, long prayer, and in some cases it will be at a scheduled time as morning or an emergency situation. There may be people who will ask you to pray for them when you least expect it but know that God is listening to you each time you call on Him. No matter what is going in your life, never stop praying. It's good to have communication with God.

But you, when you pray, go into your room, and when you have shut your door, pray to your Father who is in the secret place; and your Father who sees in secret will reward you openly. Matthew 6:6 New Kings James Version (NKJV)

# Forgive me

No one is perfect, but God. Sometimes we make mistakes and we apologize to people when we do something wrong. There are times when we know that we weren't supposed to do or say something and we ask for forgiveness from people. God wants to forgive us for our sins also, but we must ask Him. Repentance is important to God and it should be important to us. In prayer we should always repent and also if you do something and realize it was wrong (not of God) you should repent which comes from the heart and out of your mouth. People don't like to keep having to forgive someone for the same thing and God is the same way. Although God is a forgiven God we should try to stay away from, work on, stop, fix, whatever it is that is not pleasing to God. He knows that we are not like Him and need His forgiveness.

# Baptism

Only God can renew you, cleanse your sins white as snow, and give you a fresh start. On August seventeen two thousand fourteen I was baptized and I felt renewed. I was born again and filled with the Holy Spirit. I was given the chance by God to turn from my old self and start over the right way, in the light with Him. Some people receive the gift of speaking tongues, some don't immediately but do later. Some feel something different about them. Although it wasn't seen physically, internally I felt as if the darkness, the dirt and filth on the inside was washed clean of me. No matter what you feel know that you have been cleansed by the blood of Jesus. You no longer are the person you were before you were baptized.

But if we walk in the light as He is in the light, we have fellowship with one another, and the blood of Jesus Christ His Son cleanses us from all sin. 1 John 1:7

And He said to them, "Go into all the world and preach the gospel to every creature. He who believes and is baptized will be saved; but he who does not believe will be condemned. And these signs will follow those who believe: In My name they will cast out demons; they will speak with new tongues; they will take up serpents; and if they drink anything deadly, it will by no means hurt them; they will lay hands on the sick, and they will recover." Mark 16:15-18 New King James Version (NKJV)

Then Peter said to them, "Repent, and let every one of you be baptized in the name of Jesus Christ for the remission of sins; and you shall receive the gift of the Holy Spirit. Acts 2:38   New King James Version (NKJV)

# God is the Father, Son, and Holy Spirit

Have you ever felt something on the inside telling you to go somewhere or not, do something or not, say something or not? However, you did it anyway and realized you should have just listened to your gut, intuition, that feeling that came over you that would have saved you from whatever you then had to deal with. The Holy Spirit is God and you shall receive and have this gift which is a leader, comforter, teacher, guider, protector, and will never do harm to you. You should be filled with the Holy Spirit once you repent and are baptized.

One day my brother asked me to accompany him to New York for some food and the Holy Spirit told me not to go. I waited three hours before responding to him that I would go. I made many excuses up in my mind on why I should go even though the Holy Spirit told me not to go. What was supposed to be an hour ride and cost thirty dollars became seven hours and cost two hundred and ten dollars. Listen to the Holy Spirit at all times, if your feel like going left and the Holy Spirit says go right, go right! Never go against God it will never be good for you.

But the Helper, the Holy Spirit, whom the Father will send in My name, He will teach you all things, and bring to your remembrance all things that I said to you. John 14:26 New King James Version (NKJV)

Jesus answered, "Most assuredly, I say to you, unless one is born of water and the Spirit, he cannot enter the kingdom of God. John 3:5 New King James Version (NKJV)

On the last day, that great day of the feast, Jesus stood and cried out, saying, "If anyone thirsts, let him come to Me and drink. He who believes in Me, as the Scripture has said, out of his heart will flow rivers of living water." John 7:37-38 New King James Version

# Peace

Have you ever had so many things going on in a day and felt overwhelmed? Have you ever felt you were being pulled in many directions at the same time? Have you ever burned out at work or school?

God wants you to have peace within yourself a peace that He gives to you. Peace is when all negative things around can be going on and you are calm and relaxed resting in peace knowing God is within you. I have had times when things were going on personally and professionally, I know that the only way I had peace is through God Himself. Sometimes we allow the enemy to make us feel stressed and anxious. At these times you should seek God and prayer. Never feel you can't go to Him about something. He takes your worries away and gives you peace. Talking to God by praying is the best thing to do, He is the one that calms your heart, mind, and your spirit through the midst of anything you may face.

Peace I leave with you, My peace I give to you; not as the world gives do I give to you. Let not your heart be troubled, neither let it be afraid. John 14:27 New King James Version (NKJV)

Be anxious for nothing, but in everything by prayer and supplication, with thanksgiving, let your requests be made known to God; and the peace of God, which surpasses all understanding, will guard your hearts and minds through Christ Jesus. Philippians 4:6-7 New King James Version (NKJV)

## God has blessed you

God has blessed you if you are reading this book. The very breathe you are taken was given to you by Him. Life is a blessing we can sometimes take for granted. Many times we thank God when He does things for us. One thing I have noticed most times people want to thank Him on Friday, but the truth is we should be thankful for every day we have breathe. I have learned to appreciate everything that He has blessed me with. The real blessings from God are not material .Your life, spouse, children, family, and friends are gifts from God. Having good health, shelter, food on your table, clothes on your back is a blessing. There are many people who are without the basic necessities and you must be thankful and be grateful to God when you have these things. If He has blessed you with employment, your own a house, car, money in your bank account, if you are able to travel, and are able to make purchases when you want, you are beyond blessed and should want to give back in some way. Just think He gave it to you, to give back and you reap what you sow good or bad so, it's better to sow good seeds. He knows your heart and expects you to give back to the Kingdom of God. Remember when you serve God you will never lack anything you need and He wants to bless you. When He blesses you it's usually beyond what you can imagine and also at a time you couldn't imagine.

Every man shall give as he is able, according to the blessing of the Lord your God which He has given you. Deuteronomy 16:17 New King James Version (NKJV)

# We are blessed to bless others

Have you ever had someone who has done something for you and made a huge impact in your life or others? God used my friend to demonstrate to me how we should bless others when we are blessed. As we began to extreme coupon I seen God work the blessing like He did before with the bread and fish (Matthew 14:13-21) New King James Version (NKJV). We gave to people in the stores where we shopped, I blessed my family, friends, people in my community, and I still had eleven months worth of product for my household. My friend's kindness and compassion trickled down to many others who she and I don't know. God took what I seen as a small blessing and magnified it for many others. God doesn't want us to store up blessings for ourselves; He wants us to give and share our blessings with others. Never feel fear, or think that He won't take care of you because He will. God won't hold back anything good from those that serve Him. If more people gave there would be less people without in this world. I feel so blessed that He chose me and my friend to bless others. He turned something I seen as a small blessing and magnified it to bless many other people.

## Better to give than receive

We are blessed by God to be a blessing to others. I used to want to save my money items, and only give back to my family members. Frequently, my church gives back to the community by giving nonperishable items to our neighbors. At my lowest I begin to give more than usual, my children and I came in from worship service one Sunday and immediately we went through our cabinets to give to others. We also contributed some of the laundry detergent knowing from my heart that it was the right thing to do. I have also given my last, even the little change I was saving, back to God. I have also had times that I couldn't give anything and I can recall crying because I wanted to give but I had no money to give. Remember God knows our hearts though and will make a way for you to give what you can. There are also other ways to give if you have nothing monetary or would like to give in abundance. You can give your time by serving the God in ministries at your church. You can also donate your time to giving back to others in your community and around the world. The best thing you can give is yourself by becoming a living sacrifice for God.

Give and it will be given to you: good measure, pressed down, shaken together, and running over will be put into your bosom. For with the same measure that you use, it will be measured back to you." Luke 6:38

# Blessings from others

God will place people in your life for a reason, some even for a season. I know he has put many people in my life to bless me in many different ways. A mom is to be treasured at all times you only get one. My mother had me when she was sixteen years old and dedicates her life to her family. My mother is the kind of person that will do anything for anyone. She is also a person that loves people. She will communicate with just about anyone who she comes in contact with and loves to help when she is able to. She enjoys doing crafts, cooking, and decorating for events.

She is my first connection on earth of love, my backbone. We all go through things in life and God blessed me to have a great mother with a beautiful heart. My mother has faced many trials throughout her life such as being healed of cancer twice. She has also been strong enough to face the trials in mine as well as my siblings life's too.

As the oldest I have always felt that I need to be responsible at all times. I felt I was the role model who had to demonstrate leadership to my siblings. The reality is I had to go through storms in life myself and experience struggles that gave me strength. There are people that will avoid you when you have no funds, but they chose to get closer to me during this time. My sister would come over to visit the children and me more often. The phone calls increased as well as the financial support she gave to us. She would bless me with paying my bills to make sure I had lights and water on in my house. There were times when I was low on gas and she would put funds in my car or in my bag. Sometimes roles change in life and you must humble yourself and be thankful. My sister and brother in law have blessed my children and I, which I'm thankful and grateful to God for them.

God has blessed me with a friend that is one of a kind. We are completely opposite except that we love each other. I have had many trials during my life and I have had her as a friend, confidant, but I consider her more of a sister. It is a blessing to have someone you can talk to and trust with personal information. She has truly been a blessing by helping me with emotional, physical, and financial support. She has also blessed me with trips in and out of the country that have allowed me to relax and also provide kingdom work. I'm grateful to God for putting her in my life.

In two thousand and fourteen I struggled financially like never before. During the time when my children were going to school was the worst because they have needs to be met and every parent wants to make sure their child has the basics. God blessed my community and we had several back to school events which I was able to receive school supplies for my children.
The Bridgeport Public school requires the children to wear a uniform which was very tough for me to purchase with no employment. I humbly, but diligently contacted every local agency I could to seek help for their uniforms. God led me to call the uniform store which gave the contact of a local church. I persistently over three weeks made about six calls before they gave me the news that I had been waiting for which was to receive gift cards to purchase uniforms for my children. The only stipulation was the cards had to be used that day and I was excited and scared at the same time. I knew my truck was on empty but I prayed to God that He would make a way for me. I was able to pick up the gift cards and go to the uniform store. I prayed my way there and cried and

praised God on my way home because I know God can do the impossible.

I remember the day my children and I had gone to return my bottles in for a refund at the local grocery store and a woman stopped me and blessed me with three garbage bags full of bottles. I thank God for sending her my way and she gave generously. This woman was also being obedient to God as she stated to me she was from another state visiting for a wedding that weekend.

I was also blessed by a receiving Holy Bible's from an international organization to go out and provide evangelism in my community. There is no greater gift than to win souls for the Kingdom of God. I'm thankful and grateful for the donation as I know that many lives and souls were affected by receiving and spreading the word of God.

The fruit of the righteous *is a* tree of life, and he who wins souls *is* wise. Proverbs 11:30 New King James Version (NKJV)

# Gifts from God

You have a purpose while you are here on earth and everyone has been blessed with a gift from God. He has blessed me with gift such as the love for people, wisdom, encouragement, and communicating. Think about it, there are things you can do naturally that others may find difficult to do and may sometimes need training on. Recognize when something flows and you enjoy it you should thank God for that gift. Your God given gift is what many people would explain being at work but it doesn't feel like you're working work because you enjoy doing it. You can also offer that gift to help others in need. Know that He gives to you to give to others. We are given gifts to serve like Jesus, so share your gift with as many people as possible. When you leave this earth you will no longer have a need to use your gifts, so give your gift life now. Give God the glory all the time for the gift when you use it because He has given it to you.

Having then gifts differing according to the grace that is given to us, let us use them: if prophecy, let us prophesy in proportion to our faith; or ministry, let us use it in our ministering; he who teaches, in teaching; he who exhorts, in exhortation; he who gives, with liberality; he who leads, with diligence; he who shows mercy, with cheerfulness. Romans 12:6-8

for to one is given the word of wisdom through the Spirit, to another the word of knowledge through the same Spirit, to another faith by the same Spirit, to another gifts of healings by the same Spirit, to another the working of miracles, to another prophecy, to another discerning of spirits, to another different kinds of tongues, to another the interpretation of tongues. 1 Corinthians 12:8-10

And God has appointed these in the church: first apostles, second prophets, third teachers, after that miracles, then gifts of healings, helps, administrations, varieties of tongues. Are all apostles? Are all prophets? Are all teachers? Are all workers of miracles? Do all have gifts of healings? Do all speak with tongues? Do all interpret? 1 Corinthians 12:28-30

And He Himself gave some to be apostles, some prophets, some evangelists, and some pastors and teachers, Ephesians 4:11 New King James Version (NKJV)

Every good gift and every perfect gift is from above, and comes down from the Father of lights, with whom there is no variation or shadow of turning. James 1:17 New King James Version (NKJV)

# Acts of Kindness

Pray for someone you know is going through something, pray for someone you don't know. People go through test and trials daily and there are those who are in need of many things such as healing, deliverance, strength, comfort, peace, joy, and most of all love.

If you can give monetarily do it, such as being in a grocery store and someone is short for their food bill but you have the money to help. Natural disasters, house fires that people are left with nothing, someone who is hungry, homeless, and those who feel abandoned.

Your smile, hug, compliments, and compassion can help someone by bringing joy to their day. You can make an impact on someone you don't know which could lead them to God. You never know when you may be the person in need, so give it's free and goes a long way. Always be friendly and give freely.

# Image of God /You are unique

God has created everything you can see, hear, touch, smell, feel, and also the things you can't imagine. I struggled with my weight for years and felt I had to make changes to my body to be happy. I have always wanted to have bigger buttocks. I tried many diets, pills, food programs, exercise but nothing seemed to work. I ended up losing weight by stress, decreasing food portions, dancing, and walking miles each day. God created you beautifully from the inside out. God sees you as beautiful/ handsome. Society can make you feel your body should be in the image of those seen in magazines, videos, billboards, and of models, singers, actors and actresses. In fact, God created you uniquely there is no other person like you in this world. Everything about you is special and in the image of Him. He sees no flaws in or on you. He loves all people in spite of your race, height, gender, sexuality, and disability, social and economical status. He doesn't make mistakes like people do, so when He created you He did it just how He wanted you to be. I took a trip to Dominican Republic in August two thousand fourteen and reality set in for me. After talking to over fifty women I discovered that many women weren't happy about their body like myself. Many of the women have had children, had trouble losing weight, bad eating habits, self-esteem issues, and mental health issues and also have suffered some form of abuse. At least one hundred of the women in one clinic I had visited received some type of plastic, cosmetic, reconstructive, maxillofacial or hand Surgery. We now in society have gotten to a place where we change our eye color and many women have turned to waist training garments. Many celebrities, models, and women don't realize the message they are sending out to young girls and women. God used my daughter to tell me I didn't need any surgery and I thought about what I would have been saying to her if I had gotten a butt surgery. It shows someone who is not truly confident with their appearance and also someone who thinks it is better to take the easiest way out. There is a natural beauty that God has given all women. We have it and should embrace and appreciate it. As a woman I will say hair weave, nails, eyelashes, body enhancements, and any other thing you add on is not of God. You can fix everything on the outside, but until you fix your inside your still broken. Looks are temporary but your soul is what God is concerned about. God wants us to love ourselves and see the beauty He has given to us.

I will praise You, for I am fearfully and wonderfully made; Marvelous are Your works, and that my soul knows very well. Psalm 139:14 New Kings James Version (NKJV)


Charm *is* deceitful and beauty *is* passing, but a woman *who* fears the Lord, she shall be praised. Proverbs 31:30 New King James Version (NKJV)

Don't be concerned about the outward beauty of fancy hairstyles, expensive jewelry, or beautiful clothes. You should clothe yourselves instead with the beauty that comes from within, the unfading beauty of a gentle and quiet spirit, which is so precious to God. 1 Peter 3:3-4 New Living Translation (NLT)

# Respect is better than attention

Many people seek and give the wrong attention from other people, but you must be careful what kind of attention you are seeking. I used to seek negative attention from men. I loved to look good on the outside by wearing tight and short clothing. I love to talk and dance, so being seductive came easy to me. I neglected and used my body as a weapon for many years. Once I surrendered to God I asked Him to use me instead of allowing myself and other people to use me for negativity. I began to notice that men started to see God in me rather than my physical body. My heart that was cleaned by God was and now that was more appealing than what was on the outside. People stopped using vulgar language in my presence and are respectful of who I am. Everything that looks good isn't good for you. Many people do other negative things for attention I now know it's better to be respected for doing good rather than being known for doing bad and looking good.

Show proper respect to everyone, love the family of believers, fear God, and honor the emperor.

1 Peter 2:17 New International Version (NIV)

# Shine the light within you

Have ever been told by someone that there is something different about you or you have a glow? I have experienced times in my life when I have been told these things, getting something new, when starting a new relationship and job. Most times we are smiling more often and begin to talk about that person or new thing we are absorbed in. I didn't understand what it really meant until I loved God. I began to love God more than anyone and everything. The more I loved God the more I talked about Him to everyone. God must always be first no matter who or what is happening in your life. God is light and the devil is dark. Can you imagine being in a room with the lights off it will be very dark and you will not be able to see, but if you have add light such as match, a candle or flashlight the room will light up. Light will always out shine darkness when you love God and are living in His will you should have the light of God shining through you. You should have joy which is given by the Lord. The world doesn't give you joy so, don't allow anyone or anything to take it from you.

Let your light so shine before men, that they may see your good works and glorify your Father in heaven. Matthew 5:16 New King James Version (NKJV)

# It's not about you

Life seemed better when it was all about me but I have found that wasn't
true. I took care of myself, my family and I felt satisfied knowing we
were all ok. Since my relationship with God has gotten closer and to a
deeper level I have learned that it isn't about me at all. Most of all I have
learned I was never taking care of myself, God was all along. Life is now
at its best! I had to put God first and then give to people instead of
putting me first. I have learned that I had to empty myself of myself and
let God fill me up. I went from being selfish to selfless and it's
rewarding. God has filled me up with His unconditional love to give to
others, many whom I will never meet.

But seek first the kingdom of God and His righteousness, and all these
things shall be added to you. Matthew 6:33 New King James Version
(NKJV)

# Humbling Yourself

My pride I could no longer hide and had to put aside. As a child my mom had received food stamps to feed my siblings and me for many years. I had never imagined that I would have to receive food stamps to feed my family. When I worked I used to avoid going to the grocery store in the beginning of the month because of the long lines, now I know why the lines were so long. My children love to eat and by the end of the month I had bare to no food left in the house. I had no choice but to humble myself go to the grocery store, stand in the lines because I needed to feed my children.

I attended an extreme couponing class to save money for groceries and non-perishables. I remember purchasing over sixty bottles of laundry detergent for twenty dollars. Free tooth brushes, hair shampoo and conditioner and many other items. I was blessed to have a friend to help me with couponing and the items I received went a long way.

I was used to buying water and soda bottles then trashing them after we were done drinking them. However, we began to save the water bottles and later return them so that we could have money for the times ahead. I will never through my money away again.

The little things I took for granted I could no longer. We could no longer eat out at fast food restaurants. I had to wash, condition and use the same hair weave to do my hair for eight months. I went without a pedicure for over a year and learned how to do my own feet.

Sometimes God will have you to give up some of the things you take for granted to humble yourself. He is God and He can give them to you and also take them from you.

Some of the most humbling times for me were when it came to my children. I had to tell them we couldn't go places we were going to before such as the mall. I couldn't provide new clothes for them on holidays like I did before. When school time came I knew they expected the best of sneakers, but I couldn't make the purchases they wanted. My children would see others with new electronics and would consistently ask for me to purchase them the same things but still I couldn't provide. As a parent you want you don't want to see your kids sad, so many times I would cry when they left my presence knowing I could do nothing about the situation, but humble myself.

I'm grateful and thankful to God for allowing me to become a humble person. I appreciate the little things I once took for granted. The process is one I never thought I had to go through, but it was all for my good. Change is for our good sometimes. The feeling of being uncomfortable and have to get out of my comfort zone was good. It showed me that I'm no better than anyone else and should always be humble and walk in humility. God gave me strength and compassion when I had stepped into the unfamiliar things. I have been with and without things, I have been the Case Manager and the Client. However, in all circumstances God was with me. I learned to walk humbly and trust God to get me through by faith.

Humble yourselves in the sight of the Lord, and He will lift you up.
James 4:10

# Can you see your reflection?

There is no reason to judge anyone on earth including your enemies or those who persecute you. Judging people is a reflection of you and not them and many times people are unable to admit that it's really themselves. I have done many things in life that I'm not proud of, but thankful that I have been through them so that I may be able to prevent or help someone else get through the same thing. Each day I become a woman getting closer to the reflection of God which means I had to stop judging people by daily asking God to give me a heart like His and emptying myself out. No one is perfect but God and we all will have to face trials in life. Some of the trials you have already faced, are facing now or will face, may be different from others around you and some will be the same. You would want someone to help you and not hurt and judge you. No one gave you the right to judge anyone else so don't. Start at this very moment to look at people and their behaviors different by becoming a blessing to them. Get into the habit of thinking how I can help this person instead of judging them. God is the only one we must answer to that will bring judgment upon us.

"Judge not, that you be not judged. For with what judgment you judge, you will be judged; and with the measure you use, it will be measured back to you. And why do you look at the speck in your brother's eye, but do not consider the plank in your own eye? Or how can you say to your brother, 'Let me remove the speck from your eye'; and look, a plank is in your own eye? Hypocrite! First remove the plank from your own eye, and then you will see clearly to remove the speck from your brother's eye. Matthew 7: 1-5 New King James Version (NKJV)

# Reap what you sow

Have you ever done something you wish you haven't or thought you would get away with it?

I'm a living witness that you won't get away with it. I was in a relationship and wasn't happy for many years and I began to cheat on my partner .I misled him and played with his feelings and he became emotionally stressed. I know now it is a very disrespectful thing to do. I began a new relationship and had no intentions to have my heart at stake again, but I did. After four years I learned I had been with someone who was living a double life. He had been involved with two women that I know of over the course of four years. I was told many lies and had my health at risk more times than I can remember. I had reaped what I had sowed and it was the worst feeling in the world. Whatever you do to people it comes back to you and sometimes worst.
 Sewing good seeds is the best thing you can do. I have sowed good seeds in life too. My harvest of those seeds uprooted in the times that I was in need. Remember sow good seeds because you reap what you sow, good or bad. Treat people how you want to be treated at all times.

Do not be deceived, God is not mocked; for whatever a man sows, that he will also reap. Galatians 6:7

# Relationships

# Single

There were periods of times in my life when I was single and didn't know what to do with myself. I found myself dating men when I should have taken time to be alone. God wants you to be with a man of God or a woman of God. When we rush the process sometimes you end up dealing with a Joker or Jezebel and not with whom God intended you to be with. God doesn't want us to fornicate nor should one be in cohabitation with someone especially one who has no intentions on being your spouse. Sometimes people go years in relationships and don't even know who they really are, let alone who their partner is. When this happens people become or then aware that they are unhappy. Sometimes God just wants you to build a relationship with Him. When we go against God we end ourselves in heartache, trouble, and in bad relationships. There are other times when God may want you all to Himself everyone believes they shouldn't be single but what about if your calling requires you to be alone and stand strong with God. If you are single I suggest you pray for God to prepare you for a spouse if that's His will for you.

But I say to the unmarried and to the widows: It is good for them if they remain even as I am; but if they cannot exercise self-control, let them marry. For it is better to marry than to burn with passion. 1 Corinthians 7:8 New Kings James Version (NKJV)

# Marriage

Marriage is a sacred union for men and women according to God. I believe many females dream of getting married and having a wedding as a young girl or even before it even comes to pass. I have often had pictures in my mind like many other females of a church, white dress family, friends and others to witness the union of marriage. I was married at the age of twenty three in a hall, by the justice of peace. I was married for almost three years and it was no fairy tale. I feel my marriage failed because it wasn't blessed by God. I wanted to be married because we had children, but we really weren't ready. This can cause lots of damage in one's life when both people aren't honest about such a serious life changing event. Many times the man or the woman just agrees to please the other and it shouldn't be that way. Marriage is supposed to be sacred and should happen before children. I continue to be asked the question by others of me being married and my answer remains the same. I will not be married unless it is blessed by God. I stand firm in belief of pre-marital counseling. I believe it is healthy for a relationship. The man I would marry would have to put God first and love God just as much as I do with all his heart because I love God with all my heart.


Now concerning the things of which you wrote to me: It is good for a man not to touch a woman. Nevertheless, because of sexual immorality, let each man have his own wife, and let each woman have her own husband. Let the husband render to his wife the affection due her, and likewise also the wife to her husband. The wife does not have authority over her own body, but the husband does. And likewise the husband does not have authority over his own body, but the wife does. Do not deprive one another except with consent for a time that you may give yourselves to fasting and prayer; and come together again so that Satan does not tempt you because of your lack of self-control. But I say this as a concession, not as a commandment. For I wish that all men were even as I myself. But each one has his own gift from God, one in this manner and another in that. 1 Corinthians 7:7 New King James Version (NKJV)

Therefore shall a man leave his father and his mother, and shall cleave unto his wife: and they shall be one flesh. Genesis 2:24 King James Version (KJV)

He who finds a wife finds a good thing and obtains favor from the Lord. Proverbs 18:22 English Standard Version (ESV)

# Divorce

Have you ever felt you were going in circles in life or on a roller coaster ride all of the time and needed to get off? I did and I made the decision to stop the circling and get off the ride before it was too late for me. One never gets married to have to get a divorce and it is one of life's hardest decisions which some people have to make and experience. It can be a hard decision to get a divorce because of many reasons. Many people don't get a divorce because of reasons such as religion, children, financial, health, lifestyle, culture, traditions, comfortability, sex, and loneliness. I was divorced in November two thousand and nine which was not an easy process. Getting divorced affects more than just the people involved especially if you have children. My divorce affected my children and others around me, but it was necessary. I wanted my children to be raised in one home by both parents. I chose divorce instead of death due to domestic violence. I wouldn't change the decision I made because I wanted to live and my children need me. No matter who judges me I realize I have to take responsibility for my decision before God. Pray to God and seek His direction before getting a divorce.

# Unhealthy Relationships

You must be aware when you are in an unhealthy relationship. Signs of unhealthy relationships are when there is no or lack of love trust, respect, honesty, communication, loyalty and most of all God. I have been in unhealthy relationships that lead to a break ups. I believe one of the most important people in a relationship is God and both people should have love for God. It's important to know the signs of unhealthy relationships such as your partner using demeaning or vulgar language towards you, insults, psychological abuse, sexist remarks, temper outbreaks, alcohol or drug abuse, jealousy, restrictions or prohibiting you from friends and family members, checking and tracking you, controlling where you go and who you communicate with, violence while intoxication or on drugs, secrets, blames other people, deceitful and lying. Some people find it hard to accept when they are in a relationship or marriage with someone of these characteristics. Sometimes other people's advice isn't the best to get, so seek guidance from God and listen to what He says because He will never give you advice to hurt you it will be for your own good.

# Parenting

# Parenting

Parenting is a gift from God to be treasured at all times. It doesn't matter if they are yours biologically or not; take parenting as a blessing from God because there are many people who wish to love a child if they could have the chance. There is no book that can actually teach you how to be a parent. Children don't come with instructions. People have children at different ages and stages in life. If you are blessed with people who have wisdom, knowledge, and understanding on how to care for a child thank God for that because most things happen when the doctors' offices are closed. If God blesses you with more than one child you will know that each one has their own personality, likes, and dislikes. Each child is different, so the needs of each child will be different such as adults.

# Teen Parent

Most sixteen year olds are into their studies, playing sports; girls are cheerleading and hanging out with their friends, talking on the phone, going to the movies and mall and even working. It is also a time when hormones began to change boys and girls into young adults. Males were approaching me as my figure began to develop and I was changing at that time. I wasn't comfortable talking to my mom about sex and I had begun to explore my sexual feelings which were no longer thought but actions. I was pregnant at the age of sixteen and although I wasn't spiritual, I was pro-life and had decided to keep my child. It was hard going to school amongst my peers, dealing with my family, his father's family's response, and also the physical and emotional things that come along with being pregnant. Like most teens I wanted to do the things my peers were doing but I couldn't. By the age of seventeen I had given birth to my oldest son which is one of my most precious gifts from God. I was still living at home with my mom which she had told me I had to finish my senior year of high school and that I would graduate if it killed her. I thank God for her love, strength, and guidance. When my baby was two months old I got a job at a fast food restaurant which I worked for seven months. I was blessed to have support of my mom to take care of my son while I was attending school and also my younger sister when I was at work at night. It wasn't easy raising a baby, going to school, studying, working, and still trying to be a teen. I matured faster than many of my friends because I had the responsibility of taking care of my child. My son's father and I ended our relationship when our son was six months. God gave me the strength I need to move on with my life.

# Single Parent

We graduated high school and he went off to college to pursue his education. I never thought I would be a single mother. However, I was and had no choice but to accept it and move on. I received cash and medical from the state for our son for twelve months. I then began to work for an amazing company that allowed me to bring my son to work and also paid me well, so I ended the help I was receiving from the state. It was great for me at the age of eighteen because I needed the money to take care of my child. I know the difficulties that come along with being a single parent. Trying to make a living, raising a child, work, missing days for doctor visits, waiting for the other parent to show up for the child and they never come, when you're sick you still must get up and perform like your normal. Often times the absent parent's side of the family may disown the child. I thank God that after my son's father had graduated from college he began to fully be in our son's life and is a great dad to this day!

God had given me strength to keep focus on raising my son and He also has blessed me with supportive family members and a few friends to get me through that period of time in my life.

# Married Mom

Seven years later at the age of twenty three God had blessed me with a son and by twenty five God had blessed me with a daughter. I was married at the age of twenty six and I knew at this time it was better to have children while married. I had wanted for my children to have what I didn't because I had always thought my life would have been different if my dad was in the house. My hope was that my children would have a better life than I did with a male figure in the home. It is easier when there are two parents raising a child in one home. My kids were able to see love from the both of us, get help with homework; there was more physically, emotional and financially support. I believe the best thing you can do if possible is to raise a child in a two parent home.

# Divorced Mom

In two thousand and nine I was divorced. I now know I had no business getting married without having God in the relationship. After being married and having help from your spouse things change with parenting. I had to put not only more physical time in but emotional too. My divorce affected my children in many ways due to domestic violence being the reason we divorced. I spent time with friends at work, but when I had gotten home I secluded myself from my family. I needed time with God and my children. The children no longer were able to see the other parent as often as they were when we were married. The communication stopped for eighteen months due to him being incarcerated. He relocated and helped support them when he felt emotionally, physically, and financially ready to. I wanted my kids to feel comfortable. I was blessed by having a Minister witness what I was going through, she had asked a Reverend to come to my home each week and meet with me. She came and prayed with me and the kids which was a blessing for us. God was giving me my strength back, so I could be the strong mom again like I was when I was single. God had also given me His strength when I was weak.

# Parent in a relationship

Being in a relationship with someone who isn't the parent of your child or doesn't have children is an experience many people will have. It takes a special man or woman to help raise another person's child or children. It can be a lot to take on a task being responsible for the well-being of a child. One has to be selfless and not selfish. One must have a heart to become a parent. I have had the experience of living with someone other than my father most of my life. My children as well have had a special person in their lives when the other parent was absent. I was blessed as a child with having my stepfather who loves my siblings and me as we were his own. My children are also blessed with a man who goes above and beyond to make sure their needs are met at all times and with no complaints. As a parent you want to make sure your kids are comfortable with your partner and your partner is comfortable too. Sometimes adults get in a relationship to be with the parent but don't love or respect the children as they should. One should accept and love the children as they do the parent of the child or children. I have had sometimes where I have had the need to call upon both of these men in my life time and neither have left my children or myself and I thank God . God has blessed me with loving men who has taken on the roles of a parent and I'm grateful to Him for that.

# Parenting Revelation

On my son's eighteenth birthday I received a revelation from God that would change my parenting. Since the age of seventeen I couldn't wait until my son turned eighteen, I wanted the negative things to come to an end with his dad and me. The lack of respect, communication, support, trust, and years of fighting over custody would end when he became an adult. We spent many years arguing about where he would reside and go to school. We could never agree on many things during the first eighteen years of his life. The one thing we had in common is we loved him and wanted the best for him. However, I felt emotional on his eighteenth birthday all the years seemed to flash before my mind. God showed me on this day that all the negativity that we did never helped our son. My son spent his eighteenth birthday incarcerated where neither one of us would be able to see him. I felt sad, hurt, guilty, ashamed, and disappointed for allowing this to happen to my son. The fact is what we did affect our son more than us. God made me realized all these years he really didn't belong to us, he belonged to God.

It is important as parents to communicate about everything concerning the child and to do what is in the best interest of the child whether you are married or separate. This requires both parents to seek guidance from each other and mainly from God.

Behold, children are a heritage from the Lord, The fruit of the womb is a reward. Psalm 127:3New King James Version (NKJV)

# Who is training your child?

God is the best example for us all, there is never going to be a better leader than Him. As parent you should know you are the first example of a leader or role model to your child / children. I wasn't always a positive role model for my children. I remember when I was smoking marijuana, listening to ungodly music, dancing provocative, using profanity, drinking alcohol, showing low self-esteem to my children through wanting to change myself, celebrating traditions of the world and around people who really didn't have my best interest at heart. When I surrendered to Jesus, I turned from many of my wicked ways. God changed my heart, attitude, behavior, and with myself changing my children also changed. My kids no longer new the latest songs that where played on the radio nor did they know the new hip hop and rap dances. They started singing gospel songs and praise dancing instead. When I stopped using profanity they began to notice and although they never used such language I noticed I was wrong to use it in their presence in the first place. My kids have seen me drink wine coolers at family functions .They had also witnessed me having social gatherings at home which I have had alcohol involved. Although I have never been an out of control drinker or alcoholic I didn't set a good example by drinking with them around me. I'm so thankful God has taken the taste of alcohol off of my tongue so He can use me. My kids have also known I had wanted to have an enhancement done to my body but God showed me it isn't necessary to do that. I have told my kids their worth and why no one needs to do such a thing to their temple. I gave each one a Bible and began to read to them and explain scripture to them .They began to ask question and were more intrigued each week. I used to bring my kids out every Halloween which they enjoyed, but I could no longer do that once I surrendered to God and His will. I have shown my kids that sometimes you have to stand alone even if everyone else doesn't want to do what is right. I was around people such as family and who I thought was friends that really didn't care about me like they should have. They stopped coming around when I stopped indulging in the behaviors that were sinful. Change isn't always easy but it is necessary and asking God for His help and strength is needed. Due to the fact I'm not perfect daily I ask God to empty me of myself and fill me up with Him. You yourself or maybe someone you know may have some demonic behaviors such as the ones I have explained or maybe different ones that a child is observing but know you can change and know that your change will affect not only yourself but the child. Children see and hear many negative things from people outside of their home .They deal with peer pressure, bullying, gangs and violence at a higher rate than when I was growing up. We as parents and adults must start leading as positive examples to the youth. We need to set examples of how they should be, not how and what society thinks or what is read or seen in a magazine or music videos. The youth should see their and know their worth and the other of kids around them should see them as positive children. They also need to know who God is from adults and they will follow. Pray for our children to be covered by the blood of Jesus as much as you can.

Train up a child in the way he should go, And when he is old he will not depart from it. Proverbs 22:6 New King James Version (NKJV)

# He is able

## Healer

God is able to do whatever He wants and that is even more of the reason you should bow down to Him. He is the King of all Kings! I have witnessed miracles, healing and deliverance. Glory to God! My aunt was hospitalized and the doctors gave her about a week to live. She had a heart infection, her lungs were infected, and her kidneys and liver had begun to shut down. She was on life support and I remember the doctors clearly asking my family and me what we think. I stated to the doctors that if it is the will of God she shall live. The doctor reluctantly agreed with my family and me. The doctor was leaving for a conference and stated we probably wouldn't see him again due to her condition. He stated usually the patient dies. Glory to God! She remained on life support for over thirty days and now is in a rehabilitation center recovering with no ventilator. God is miraculous! He is a doctor and a healer, there is nothing He can't heal.

# Provider

There was a time I recall when my gas light was below empty on my truck. I stopped at the nearest gas station with the last ten dollars I had to put in the tank. I went in the store paid ten dollars for the gas and proceeded to pump. If you have ever put ten dollars in your tank you know it doesn't take long to come out. I noticed I had been pumping for some time as I looked at the screen to my surprise it read twenty four dollars fifty four cent. I then went into the store to tell the clerk and she stated I could leave. God filled up my gas tank! I couldn't do anything but thank God because He did that. God knows what you need and He is an on time. He never fail me know that God is a provider.

# Deliverer

If you are like most people you will encounter some kind of life event, but know that you can be delivered by Jesus. I had reached a point in my life were I had almost lost my mind. It had seemed like everything was coming against me and my back was against the wall. But God delivered me from the depression I was in, He treated me. I cried many nights for God to help me, to clean my heart, take the enemy out because I knew I wasn't myself .I know there is nothing you are too deep in, that He can't deliver you from. If you have an addition to drugs, sex, shopping, cheating, stealing, lying, food, gambling, food, work, love, exercise. If you find yourself suffering from a mental health disorder such as depression and anxiety, in a place where you can't or don't want to talk to anyone pick up your Bible and call on the Lord. Jesus is near; He is closer than you may think all you have to do is call on Him. I know He can deliver you because He delivered me from many things. Know that no one on earth is perfect and we all fall short of the glory of God each day until we are delivered before Him in heaven. Each day is a new journey. You must continually ask Him to keep you covered by His blood. God is a deliverer!

The Lord is near to all who call upon Him, to all who call upon Him in truth. Psalm 145:18 King James Version (KJV)

# Protector

God has protected all people on earth since the time we were in our mother's womb. God has demonstrated His protection over my life countless times. Born and raised in Bridgeport, Connecticut which is the largest populated city in the state of Connecticut. As a child I grew up in the projects or the ghetto as some would call it. I remember a time when a bullet came through our window. I had childhood friends that were killed due to street violence. There were many single parents like my mom that wanted to get out of the projects. It was hard for my mom, but God made a way and we moved out. We moved from one urban area to another in the city. Now raising my three children I live one street from a project which has the similar things going on. God has protected my family from this violence many of times over many of years. God will also protect you from people and situations that may cause you harm.

Whoever dwells in the shelter of the Most High will rest in the shadow of the Almighty. I will say of the Lord, "He is my refuge and my fortress, my God, in whom I trust." Psalm 91 New International Version (NIV)

# Grace

To God be the glory! I'm so thankful for His grace that He has upon us each day. One of the toughest times in my life was when my daughter was eight months old. I had come home from work and she appeared to be sleeping. I went upstairs where mom lived and where one of my sons were playing at the time. Within five minutes I could hear someone screaming my name, so I went to see what was going on. Shockingly, I see my daughter in someone's arms like a doll unconscious. I asked what is going on and the reply I got was I don't know she won't wake up! I rushed down the stairs, calling her name swept her mouth and nothing. I began calling her name, slapping her face, and seeing her eyes opening and rolling, with foam around her mouth. The way God works is on time because my brother had just pulled in my driveway. I immediately got into his vehicle and ask him to bring me to the local hospital as fast as possible. We were at the hospital within five minutes. God was on time again. I felt I was watching a movie as I walked in to the Emergency room and a physician asked" what's going on?" I replied "I don't know but she is unconscious" they immediately took her from my arms and began to work on her. After running some test they confirmed she had ingested Phencyclidine (PCP or Angel dust) a hallucinogenic illegal drug. They didn't know how to treat her and her body temperature wasn't staying warm, so she had to be transferred to a hospital which was a half hour away. While in the Intensive Care Unit the doctors stated she almost died three times that night. My spirits were low, but God had grace and mercy on her soul. My son had to stay in a foster home one night as I stayed with my daughter in ICU. She remained in the hospital for a week. After the State of Connecticut Department of Children and Families investigation and a court appearance I got my children back in my home. For the next six months I would have to deal with having the State of Connecticut Department of Children and Families in my life over something I didn't do. I thank God for His grace and mercy over my children even when they weren't in my care they were in His all the time.

And He said to me, "My grace is sufficient for you, for My strength is made perfect in weakness." Therefore most gladly I will rather boast in my infirmities, that the power of Christ may rest upon me. 2 Corinthians 12:9 New King James Version (NKJV)

# Forgiver

At the age of eighteen and with a child under the age of one I was
pregnant for the second time. I was still living at home with my mom
who was helping me raise my son, so the last thing I had wanted to tell
her is, I was pregnant again. Even though I wasn't attending church at
the time I knew that having a baby was a blessing from God and I was
pro-life which made my decision very hard. My relationship with my
son's father had ended by the time I had found out I was pregnant and he
was away in college. I contacted him several times because I had wanted
to keep the baby or give it up for adoption but he pleaded for me to
terminate my pregnancy. I waited until I was three months pregnant until
I decided to have an abortion. It was a horrible experience from the
beginning to the end that I will never forget. There were religious people
outside holding signs of pictures with fetus's and scripture on it, telling
you were wrong for going to have an abortion and also people from
community programs offering assistance to help you if you would
change your mind. It looked and sounded good for the moment but I
knew I had to keep moving forward with it. I remember sitting in the
waiting room with my friend who was caring for my son and other
women with their support system who had an appointment for the
procedure that day. After saying goodbye to them I had to go through a
series of questions regarding my physical and mental health they also
explained how they would perform the procedure. One of the most
painful things was to have an ultrasound and see the baby. The fact that I
was in my second trimester, I had to have a cervical dilation which took
three hours before I could have the procedure. I can still remember
waiting in an area before being called and hearing the sound of the
woman before me having her baby sucked out of her. After I had the
procedure I left the building with birth control and lots of emotional
feelings. I had to go home as if nothing happened knowing my mom

would have been furious. I cried in the shower for weeks because I felt very guilty for what I had done. I knew it was not of God. Since then I have had two children and a tubal ligation.

# Domestic Violence

Domestic violence is an epidemic affecting individuals in every community, regardless of age, economic status, sexual orientation, gender, race, religion, or nationality a fraction of a systematic pattern of dominance and control. Domestic Violence includes physical violence, sexual violence, threats, and emotional abuse Domestic violence can result in physical injury, psychological trauma, and in severe cases, even death. The devastating consequences of domestic violence can cross generations and last a lifetime.

Domestic Violence has been in the media more since professional athletes have assaulted their partners. No matter who you are, you have no right to put your hand or objects on anyone and no one has to stand for that. Know that you always have a choice to leave and there is help for both the victim and the abuser.

I never thought I would be in a domestic violence relationship, but I was for two months. After having two black eyes, a broken nose, and many bruises it ended quickly for me. Domestic violence also affected my children not physically but they experienced living with me after the assault. I thank God because He is the Father of my home. You can always call on God. I cried out to God and comforted me and He gave me strength to carry on. I will never be silent about this issue knowing many people remain silent for years or even end up dying due to the abuse. I'm not a victim, I'm a survivor of domestic violence.

Having known people who are currently in domestic violence relationships and also people who are survivors of domestic violence I continue to pray because love doesn't hurt and God can heal their wounds. No one deserves to be abused no matter what is going on or has happened. I also pray for the abuser who needs help too. Many times people are focused on the victim and then the abuser commits abuse in a future relationship. God is wants to help all people involved and He can deliver demons from the abuser.

# Alcohol

Alcohol has affected me throughout my life in many ways. I love my family member in spite of the things he has gone through in life. My closest relative was the first person I seen abuse alcohol. Alcohol addiction is very harmful to a person and others around them. He would drink and become a different person, his personality and behavior would change. My relative loves music which I do too, but I was put in situations I shouldn't have been in because of his love for music and my concern for his safety such as getting in the car with him while he was drunk. I remember him driving and being intoxicated to the point that he almost hit a pedestrian and was angry with the pedestrian who did nothing wrong. There was also a time when he was attempting to enter into the highway where others were supposed to be exiting. He would drink enough till he blacked out and couldn't remember what had happened the day or night before. One day I had enough courage to tell him he was an alcoholic and he became upset with me and denied it. I knew then I had to be mindful of using alcohol because I never wanted it to take me over in such ways. I thank God for His love, grace, mercy, protection, and deliverance over my relative's life. God had cleansed and delivered him when he was incarcerated and keeping him for His will. Alcohol addiction is very harmful to a person and others around them. Never let anyone risk your safety for their behaviors. You can always seek God for deliverance.

# Crack

One of the worst things to do is watch someone you love suffer due to substance abuse. One of my relatives which is one of my favorite people in the world; I have witnessed her addictions to many drugs for over twenty years crack being one of them. I witnessed her sober and clean over the years when she went into rehabilitation and incarceration, but for most of her life she ran the streets to get a high. She has many gifts and talents but they weren't useful due to her drug abuse. Crack made her a different person and changed her life. At the age of eight she left me in her house with her younger two children for two days while she was out getting high. She neglected to raise her children because she was dependent on using drugs and could no longer care for them the way she should. She would steal money from me and other valuables from our family to get high. Crack and other drugs kept her away from our family from time to time. Most of the people she ran with in the streets died long ago due to AIDS .She realized she missed out on many things due to her drug abuse. She had pleaded for forgiveness not only from the family but from God. I know God had mercy on her soul when she was hospitalized then accepted Jesus as her Lord and was miraculously lived.

# Marijuana

My experience with marijuana was first as an adolescent. I would smoke it with my friends occasionally but found it easy to quit. I was forced to quit at one point in time when my children were at risk due to the other parent and child services were involved which never bothered me. However, the last time I was using marijuana I found myself to the point I acknowledged I was addicted. I started using small doses and when I felt stressed out I would use it in such a large dose thinking it would make my pain go away. I know people use it recreationally, but I used it as self-medication. I used marijuana several times a day and was highly emotional to the point I didn't feel the side effects of marijuana anymore. All of my problems were still there after I had used marijuana and concluded I was at a greater lost than the drug itself. Mentally I was in pain and I lost time with my children, family, friends, and financially I had no right wasting my finances the way I did on marijuana. I started seeing everything before me clearly; my usage was out of control and also the people who would come around me only to smoke. I started to reduce my smoking one day at a time. One day God woke me up and I no longer had the urge to smoke marijuana I have been in environments with people who smoke marijuana and now I testify how God delivered me and broke my addiction from marijuana and if He did it for me He can do it for them if they wanted Him to also.

## Pills

I suffered from depression and insomnia due to domestic violence and I was prescribed sleeping pills that I took regularly to help me sleep during the night. I found myself even more depressed when in another relationship and when this happened I began to take the pills more often along with smoking marijuana. I would come home from work, cook for my family, and as soon as the kids went to sleep I would take a pill. I tried to block out the reality of what I was dealing with in my relationship. I felt sleeping would make my situation disappear and I would have another day to face what was going on tomorrow instead of dealing with them then. The time came when I no longer was able to see my doctor due to health insurance changes which also ended my usage of sleeping pills. I'm thankful to God for His love, grace, and mercy on my life I could have been dead but God had a plan for my life.

## Boasting

I'm not proud of the things I have done, but I'm thankful and grateful to God for His love, mercy, grace, protection, and forgiveness that He has for me. I lived of the world and when I did, I indulged in it. I now live in the spirit in the world. For God, I give my all by going in my hardest, knowing I'm doing right I ask Him to use me for His will each day. If I boast it will be in the Lord. Don't get discouraged because of your past. Never be afraid to talk to anyone about God and keep in mind He is with you.

But God forbid that I should boast except in the cross of our Lord Jesus Christ, by whom the world has been crucified to me, and I to the world. Galatians 6:14 NKJV

## Temptation and testing

Once you stop doing something that was not of God you will be led by temptation and you must resist it. I used to smoke marijuana regularly and once I gave it up I was tempted many times. I was offered free marijuana when I gave it up which was very unlikely to happen because any other time the people would have never gave me any free marijuana, but I refused to take it. I was in environments around people who would began to start smoking and had to refuse and sometimes I had to also remove myself from the environment. There was a time I had been walking in the park regularly with some other people who wanted to lose weight but one day while we were walking in the park I came across a bag of marijuana. I immediately knew it was uncommon to happen and I also knew it was a test. It took me sometime but I discarded the bag of marijuana.

There will be times when you will be tempted when you are feeling weak, but again resist. Many of times I had to pray, fast, rebuke, call a friend for distraction, remove myself from the environment, and think of why I quit the behavior. Once you make it up in your mind you want to change be prepared to be in situations and prepare yourself on things you can do. God will not tempt you but Satan will. God will test you and the best thing to do is go to Him especially if you are weak. I knew many times only God could help me. I know I was weak, but I also know God is stronger and more powerful.

Let no one say when he is tempted, "I am tempted by God"; for God cannot be tempted by evil, nor does He Himself tempt anyone .James 1:13 New King James Version (NKJV)

Therefore submit to God. Resist the devil and he will flee from you. James 4:7 New King James Version (NKJV)

## Being a strong soldier

I never thought I would have to become a soldier for God, but I found out during my journey that you must be a soldier. Just as a soldier that fights against wars, you will have to fight too. The fight isn't for against people but against evil and demonic spirits that prey especially on the weak. Just like a soldier has to be trained by going to basic training you will have to be trained also. God will test you and he will stretch you for His purposes. Soldiers are armed with defense tools and you must be too. You should have your full body armor of God on which is your breastplate of righteousness, your shield of faith, your helmet of salvation, your sword of the spirit, and your feet protected by the gospel of peace. As on the battlefield the strong soldiers are the ones who stand guard and are harder to attack. Sometimes you can get caught up with things going on in the world which pull you away from God. When this happens you get weak and weak is not where you want to be. You have to put in effort to stay connected to God at all times. You must be ready, equipped, and strong for the battle!

For we do not wrestle against flesh and blood, but against principalities, against powers, against the rulers of the darkness of this age, against spiritual *hosts* of wickedness in the heavenly *places.* Ephesians 6:12 New King James Version (NKJV)

# God heals better that time

My relationship with my father was good at the time I was the age twenty but one call would change my feelings for a long time. On a Friday he disclosed to me that I would hear things about him that wasn't true ;I asked him what would I hear but he never said he just stated what I will hear isn't true about him. On the following Monday I had received a phone call with information stating he was arrested for having sex with a minor. She was twelve years old and had been pregnant with his child. I was also told she had gone for an abortion, the worst part is I knew who she was. This incident affected relationships in my family. It took a couple of years before he contacted me while he was incarcerated and he tried to explain what happened, but I didn't want to hear it at the time. I struggled with my emotions as he called me three times during the six years he was incarcerated. I always told my father I loved him at the end of each call knowing that I was emotionally torn. I was hurt, disgusted, embarrassed, ashamed, angry, and disappointed. I felt let down by the man that I believed should have set a positive example for my siblings and me. After he was released from being incarcerated for six years he resided in a shelter across from my apartment which was very different for me to be that close to him. I tried my best to help him get back on his feet and showing him love. The outside of me didn't reflect what was happening on the inside. I held on to what had happened which resulted in me losing trust for him. I struggled with the fact of him not owning up to what he had done. He tried placing the blame on everything but him such as alcohol and the minor child.

I tried to connect with him as much as possible but I have three children and I felt uncomfortable with him around my children. My father surrendered to Jesus while he was incarcerated and changed his life. God showed me his consistency with his change because he demonstrated his life as new with letting go of old things and behaviors. God had also reminded me of forgiveness and judging people. I could no longer hold on to any of the feelings I had for years. God forgave him for everything so who was I to judge him for what was forgiven from God. I knew God had forgiven me for things I've done too. God healed my heart, not time.

# Death

# Losing of a loved one

My first experience with losing a loved one is when my grandmother passed away. She was an active grandparent that I was around each week .She was sixty six years old and it was a painful process for me. I remember the ambulance workers coming to get her from her house a few times and visiting her in the hospital, but I didn't know what was wrong with her. The adults in the family told the kids she was sick. I recall the day my mom told us she was going to die, but I didn't understand all the details about people dying at this time either as her time was closer than I could imagine. It was the beginning of December the holidays were approaching and she was in the hospital. I asked mom to take us for a visit and she said she would bring my siblings and I the following day. In the middle of the night I was awakened by my mom screaming no, in a tone of voice I had never heard from her before. Tomorrow never came for me to see her I carried that for a long time the feeling of not being able to say goodbye .My grandmother had cancer and I realize now it was even more painful for her knowing and accepting the fact that she was going to die, leaving her loved ones, the pain from the cancer killing her from the inside out. She suffers no more because she was called home to be with God in peace. I thank God for the time I had with my grandmother she was a beautiful woman inside out and I treasure her love she gave to me.

Do not boast about tomorrow, for you do not know what a day may bring forth. Proverbs 27:1 New King James Version (NKJV)

My maternal grandparents were really close to me and I thought losing my grandmother was difficult at the age of twelve. When my grandmother was called home to be with the Lord my grandfather moved in with us. My grandfather was like the father I never had. He was the kind of man that took care of his responsibilities. He owned his own business, loved to travel, but loved his family more than everything else. He was a man that would tell wise stories and make you laugh. He was the first one to talk to me about death in depth and I felt relieved to have an understanding about the process. The most memorable thing he did was teach me about love. I love the way he loved my grandmother for over forty years and I had only seen him cry one time and that's when she passed away. He loved his children, grandchildren, family, friends, and others around him. He loved to listen to love songs .His favorite artist was Luther Vandross. He would sing Luther's songs often and I knew although my grandmother passed he would be thinking of her at those times. He lived with us for almost fifteen years until the day he had a sudden heart attack and was called to be with the Lord. We had no preparation it happened so quickly.

It was a hot summer day in July when I received a phone call that my cousin had been killed. I have known many people to lose their life due to violence, but this was the first time it had happened to someone I was close to in my family. I felt like I was in a movie, watching people surround the crime scene tape, screaming and weeping, police detectives surrounding where his body laid, comments that were on social media, rest in peace shirts with his face on them, and family members weeping in pain. I felt numb and my heart was weary for everyone that was affected. Most of all I pray for God to be with his parents as I could never imagine losing a child and the pain that they felt. My memories of my cousin and I will always be in my heart as from time to time I think of our childhood and great times we had.

In two thousand and fourteen I had been volunteering at a senior center for some time. God had placed a special woman in my life. I would sit, talk, and do her nails during the time I was there. Some weekends I would bring my children to see her and attend bingo with her for company. God had stretched my heart beyond the capacity that I could ever imagine. I would bring her pants home to hem them. I remember she stained her favorite blouse which I brought home and removed the stain out of. She would sing and tell me her feelings and I enjoyed listening to her stories. I would go to the stores to pick up items she wanted, help her with her make -up, and curl her hair. I never met any of her loved ones, but made every attempt to make her happy for the time she was there. I was shocked to receive the phone call from the home when she went off to be with God. I never got a chance to say goodbye to her although she would always tell me how much she appreciated the things I did for her. I also appreciated all she had to offer me. I knew God had put us in each other's life for a short season but for many great reasons. He knew she was going to need assistance so He put us together. God gave me strength, guidance, and resources to meet her needs.

Losing a love one is never easy to deal with, but it is something we all will have to deal with during our lifetime on earth. Everyone deals differently and grief's differently when death occurs. It doesn't matter if it's long suffering, sudden, violent or natural it hurts. It doesn't matter if one is old, young, a family member or friend it hurts. I don't even ask what the cause of death is anymore because the most important thing to know is if the person accepted Jesus as their Lord and Savior. Everything else was already written by God. In some cases such as my friend I met in the elderly home we became closer than some of my family members and me. You never know when it will be the last time you will see or talk to someone, so it's best to give love whenever you get the chance. I couldn't have gotten through all of these deaths without God. When people leave or stop calling to check on you remember God is always there. You can lay your burdens on Him. God will comfort, strengthen, heal your pain, and love you through the time of losing a loved one.

We are confident, yes, well pleased rather to be absent from the body and to be present with the Lord. 2 Corinthians 5:8 New King James Version (NKJV)


Blessed are they that mourn: for they shall be comforted. Matthew 5:4 King James Version (KJV)

# Shaken for a purpose

A wise woman once told me the Lord will take everything from you to get your attention. I didn't want to believe this at the time but it was sure to come true for me. I had no employment at the time my son was seventeen and like many teenagers he wanted to test himself outside in the world. He grades dropped, he was skipping school, abusing drugs, and kept himself in a negative environment. He was warned by his parents and many family members of the negative things in the world, but refused to listen to anyone. One Sunday after church I was notified to come to the police station where he was held. At this time I could not save him anymore. As a parent one of the hardest kinds of love to give is tough love but sometimes it needs to be done. It was the toughest times in my life not being able to see my son off to his prom and graduate high school with his class, but it was all a part of God's plan. While he was in prison he made a choice to attend school. God then performed a miracle for him. Glory to God! To my surprise I received a call from his high school that he hadn't been to for the last three months to pick up his High school diploma and transcript for college. Six months later many of the boys that my son was in the street with were in prison. Some were incarcerated for small crimes and a few for murder. I will never forget the day my son told me he began to pray with other inmates and he would lead prayer some nights. God had begun a work on Him to save him for a purpose. God had saved him to receive his diploma, kept him off the streets which saved his life. Most of all His purpose was to start a relationship with God for His will.

# Who do you serve?

All of my life I have had the desire to be successful. I had believed the
only way to do so is to earn lots of money, become wealthy and have
material things. I had been working since the age of fifteen with the
desire to one day not have to work really hard to support my family. I
have been blessed to work with preschool aged children, teenagers,
adults, and the elderly population. I have worked with people who have
mental health, substance abuse, and physical health issues. I have worked
with people of many different races, social, and economical
backgrounds. After being laid off from a job I worked for over ten years
and my unemployment benefits being exhausted I had thought I found
the perfect opportunity. I had wanted to work for a company that offered
residual income which allowed me to travel around the world. Knowing
how much I love to travel and having all the qualifications to recruit
clients I felt it was a great match. However, I watched others succeed and
I had gotten nowhere. Many of the people I tried to enroll I had to deny
because their country wasn't on the approval list. Most of the meetings
were held on Tuesdays, which was the same day and time as worship
service. The Holy Spirit led me to go to worship services instead of the
meetings. I had made a choice that I had to serve God completely and not
worry about how I would receive income. It was a process that had taken
place for six months before I surrendered. I was required to pay a
monthly membership which many months I had been blessed by others
that paid it for me. God told me He is over the world not the company
that claimed to be venturing the world. I used to

believe success meant money and material things but I have learned that is not true. Success is when you serve God by doing His will.

"No one can serve two masters. Either you will hate the one and love the other, or you will be devoted to the one and despise the other. You cannot serve both God and money. Matthew 6:24 NIV (New International Version)

# He's calling you

God was calling me for many years and I refused to surrender because I felt I wasn't ready. He used many people and circumstances to get my attention I wish I had listened to Him sooner.

God blessed me with my grandmother Dorothy Riley Belle she along with my mother was the first woman to bring me into the house of God. Every Saturday I would go get my hair pressed at a local salon, she would then have beautiful dresses and shoes for me to wear for the next day. We would go to church were there were lots of women, men, and children all dressed up and happy to see us come. The Pastor preaching the gospel, the gospel choir singing, women that wore big hats, tambourines in our hands, church fans that cooled us down, the people clapping and shouting, and the food after the service downstairs made me want to come back every week. My grandmother loved to cook, so after service we would go home and enjoy a big Sunday dinner. Oh how I loved Sundays! I attended church with her until she became ill and returned to God.

God has placed a special woman in my life that has left a positive mark in my heart for the rest of my life. For over ten years I would watch her grow spiritually .She has a passion to help other people and like most days she encouraged everyone around her to do the same. I would get very weary at times when she would come around my space talking about Jesus. She would have me go to churches to pray, a gospel radio station, present education, serve, and most of all to spread love to people. I will never forget the time she anointed my space with oil. I was thinking what made her do such a thing? (Now I know she was praying for us) She would often tell me stories from the Bible that would intrigue my soul, but I could never tell her that because at the time I was not ready to submit to God. During the time I was going through a divorce she reached out to another woman to come in my home to meet with me weekly and build my spirits back up. After my divorce I moved to another house which she came to bless. She also held a service in my backyard one summer which family, friends, and community member were invited too. She reminded me that Jesus knows my address that He knew where I was. She has always encouraged me to go beyond what I see and to remain faithful to the Lord. I felt she was supposed to be trying to help people save their live but she wanted to save lives and souls for God.

God truly blessed me with a beautiful daughter and placed her in my life for many reasons. Since the age of five she would ask me to go to church and I would refuse to go. She would sometimes accompany me to work functions and services that took place in a church. I just wasn't there yet. Often times she would ask other people such as my mom and sister to take her along with them, which they would. Some days my spirit would be down knowing I should have bought her to church myself. Now at the age of nine I'm proud to say she has gotten to see her mom love God more than anything else. I believe God has a calling for my daughter as every time we go to worship service she is in tune to the word of God and loves to be in the house of the Lord. God will use children.

God has placed a man in my life that has loved God since we were teenagers. He is a friend of mine but more of a brother. We all need a friend we can talk to about anything and in this journey I have been blessed. He was the only one that I could talk to about God for over five minutes without wanting to hang up the phone. Although He lives over five hundred miles from me, he came to see me baptized and just the fact that he gives me his ear, opens his heart, prays for me and we pray together is a blessing. He embraces me for who God says I am and becoming. He doesn't judge me by my past , he genuinely has touched my heart by having love and compassion just like God .I find the most valuable things in life are priceless and they can't be measured or paid back. I'm blessed by God to have a friend such as him. I believe we all need someone who we can count on during good and bad times; that person that can keep us connected to God if they see or hear us getting off track. Having someone to talk to about your spiritual health is a blessing we all deserve to have whether it's a family member, friend, or someone in your church. No one should have to feel alone.

# The plan

Before you even born in to the world your parents may have had a plan for your life. When I was a child my mom had a plan for my life. I was expected to finish elementary, middle, high school and then graduate college. She then planned I would have a successful career, the fact that I'm a female she had planned for me to get married and have children. I then had employers who had their plan for me as to see where I would grow within their organization or company. My siblings, friends, family members, coworkers also had plans, ideas, and visions as to how my life would or should go. I have had my own plans in which some came to pass and others didn't. I'm so thankful to God for not giving me what I have asked for all of the time because He knew it wasn't right for me .Know that you are being molded daily, God has had a plan for my life as well as yours all along from the time you were in your mother's womb until the time you will be in His presence.

# Your assignment

The assignment I received from God was not what I could ever imagine. I was given the assignment to speak to the world about Him in different languages on a social media site. I began to tweet scriptures from the Bible in forty two languages each morning. I only speak one language fluently which is English. However, God gave me the resources to complete the assignment. You may receive an assignment that doesn't make sense. You may be thinking to yourself how am I going to do this? I was also given the assignment to pray and give Bibles out .I had no money but God put the right people in my life at the right time that blessed me with Bibles. I'm telling you to ask God and always remember if it's an assignment from God He will provide every resource you need. I then began spreading the word of God to as many people as I could each day. I had often wondered why God allowed me to experience many things in life. I realize that if I didn't go through the trials I wouldn't have a testimony for others to know if He did it for me He will do it for you. I have also wondered why God chose to use me when I felt broken down at the time. I now know that no one is ever too lost to the point where they can't be saved and were they can't be used by God. He wants to use us all for a great purpose of His will. I have had times were people have tried to get me away from the assignments God had given to me , but when I notice it happening I refocus quickly. Never let anyone or anything stop you from the assignment God has given you. God's agenda should always come first and if you feel yourself backsliding from it pray and never be afraid to call on the name of Jesus.

# Trust God

Trusting God is not as easy as it sounds. I had been what I thought was an independent woman and I had the control. I consider myself an analytical person for the most part but I quickly found out you can't analyze God. There were times I couldn't trust myself, I said I wouldn't do things but I would later do them. It took me sometime and failures to fully trust God and not myself. God will sometimes put you in situations to test you. He can take everything from you, so you have no choice but to trust Him. I realized I had no control at all and I was out of control before I found out God has all of the control. Most people believe that they have a secret that no one knows about, but the truth is you can hide things from people however you can't hide them from God. He sees, knows and hears everything. The thoughts on your mind and even your heart He knows about, the words that come from your mouth even when you are in a place with no one physically present, God hears. He sees when you do anything there is no hiding from Him. He knew everything about you before you were even created, He knows what you're going through and He has the power to handle your situation the best way possible. Trusting in God is the best thing you can do for yourself. He wants to be your best friend if you allow Him in your heart and soul. We are in the now but God knows the end of our life.

Trust in the LORD with all your heart, and lean not on your own understanding; In all your ways acknowledge Him, and He shall direct your paths.  Proverbs 3:5-6 New King James Version (NKJV)

Trust God from the bottom of your heart; don't try to figure out everything on your own. Listen for God's voice in everything you do, everywhere you go; he's the one who will keep you on track. Don't assume that you know it all. Run to God! Run from evil!

Your body will glow with health, your very bones will vibrate with life! Honor God with everything you own; give him the first and the best. Your barns will burst, your wine vats will brim over. But don't, dear friend, resent God's discipline; don't sulk under his loving correction. It's the child he loves that God corrects; a father's delight is behind all this. Proverbs 3:5-12 The Message (MSG)

# Doing your part

It is important to have faith in God. Believing and knowing that He is going to come through for you is required but know that it doesn't happen by doing nothing. For example this book I'm writing now I had to have faith in God that He will work it out to be published and read by readers. However I had to do my part which is writing the book itself. Many times we want God to work out a miracle for us while we sit back and do nothing, while God needs us to do our part too. You may be in a situation where you are looking for employment which means you should be applying, so God can open the door for you. You may be in need of food which means you need to go and sign up for assistance, go to a local food pantry, humble yourself and tell someone that knows the resources to get you food. You may have to end relationships to allow the one God has for you to start. You must have faith in God of the unseen that it will be done.

Faith without works is dead! What does it profit, my brethren, if someone says he has faith but does not have works? Can faith save him? James 2:14 New King James Version (NKJV)

So Jesus said to them, "Because of your unbelief; for assuredly, I say to you, if you have faith as a mustard seed, you will say to this mountain, 'Move from here to there,' and it will move; and nothing will be impossible for you. Matthew 17:20 New King James Version (NKJV)

# Be still in God's time

There are other times in life when you must be still and know that God is God all by Himself. He has all power and authority over everything on earth and heaven .Sometimes we try to do things that God doesn't want us to such as me applying for employment when He wanted me to focus on Him. It didn't matter how much education, experience, or people I knew I couldn't get but so far unless He allowed me to. The closer I came to God I knew the door would open when He wanted to open it .You may be trying to do something that won't seem to move such as a new position at work, buying a home or car .You may also believe you are ready to end or start a new relationship or marriage. God doesn't work like we do everything is on His time when we He is ready. In the meantime ask Him what you could do. I didn't get employment but I was able to continue school.

To everything *there is* a season, a time for every purpose under heaven:  A time to be born, and a time to die; a time to plant, and a time to pluck *what is* planted; a time to kill, and a time to heal; a time to break down, and a time to build up; time to weep, and a time to laugh; a time to mourn, and a time to dance; a time to cast away stones, and a time to gather stones; a time to embrace, and a time to refrain from embracing; a time to gain, and a time to lose; a time to keep, and a time to throw away; time to tear, and a time to sew; a time to keep silence, and a time to speak; time to love, and a time to hate; a time of war, and a time of peace.  Ecclesiastes 3:1-8 New King James Version(NKJV)

Be still, and know that I am God; I will be exalted among the nations, I will be exalted in the earth! Psalm 46:10New King James Version (NKJV)

# Never give up

Have you ever felt as you ever felt the weight of the world on your shoulders? Have you ever been led to do something stopped? Has someone ever made you feel you weren't qualified to do something you are passionate about? Have you gave up on something due to the time and or cost?

When a baby is learning to walk, it falls and some cry, scream, kick, stumble, and some stay down for a minute, but the baby gets back up and walks. Jesus went through it also He was ridiculed, lied on, beaten, died but He rose again and He lives! We have times too, but no matter what may have you down, get up, rise, call on the name of Jesus, put on your full body armor of God, and walk.

Many times in life we give up easily for many reasons and we shouldn't. You will face many challenges when you are in the will of God, but you must continue to move forward. The enemy will try to stop you, but God will defeat him every time. Remember God has never lost a battle! I was beginning to spread the word of God through social media and at first things were going smoothly and then the enemy tried to attack what God had set out for me to do. My battery to my laptop had gotten a shortage, then it became damaged but God blessed me with another one. After that my screen went and I had no funds for another one but God provided me with resources to continue to complete the assignment.

I believe education is important to have. At an early age my mom told me that once you learn something no one can take it away from you. Most people go to school to earn an Associate's degree and complete the program within two years. It had taken me ten years to earn a two year degree. I had circumstances and situations along the way which many people face in life. I had a marriage, divorce, three children, full time job, unemployed, complications with my financial aid, domestic violence, depression, and drug abuse, children taken away, and hospitalized. There were times when I took breaks from school. I have had to walk in the heat and snow, but I never gave up. I knew God would give me His strength if I asked Him to in order to keep moving forward. Remember God will not give up on you, so don't give up on Him.

# He is always worthy

God is always worthy to be praised and worshipped. Many people tend to praise the Lord when times are good but what happens when they aren't going the way you want them too. People wouldn't believe that I worshipped and praised God when I was at my lowest. I had no employment, no money to pay my bills, my child was incarcerated, no food in my house at times, no gas in my car, but I know He is worthy at all times. He is worthy when you have and when you don't have. Remember you are always blessed not because of what you have but because of who you belong to. We could never repay God for what He has done for us. God sacrificed His only son Jesus for us, He takes our burdens, defeats our enemies. I remain in love and focused on Jesus to this day just because of who He is.

God is Spirit, and those who worship Him must worship in spirit and truth." John 4:24 New King James Version (NKJV)

# Let Go and let God

Truth is when you made the choice to accept Jesus you also made the choice for God to make necessary changes in your life .Change isn't always easy for people to do and accept. We as people tend to get uncomfortable and put up a fight when things change. God sometimes wants us to release people and things in our life for Him to do what He wants to do with us. I had a friendship with someone for several of years that I believed at the time was one worth saving although God had a different plan. I thought I would be able to help her mature as a woman and mother because I was older and had experience. Unexpectedly things changed and God revealed to me why this friendship had to end. I realized not everyone is meant to be in your life and God will end relationships by showing you people if you ask Him to or not. It can be even more difficult to end a relationship with a partner but you must come to a reality of what the relationship is doing to you physically, emotionally, and spiritually. God wants to do some work on you and He can't do it if you are doing negative things or being around negative people. Releasing some things and people has been the best thing God has done for me.

# My prayer for you

Father, I love you, I thank you, and would like to magnify your name as most high. Father please forgive me for any sins I have committed. Thank you for your love, grace, and mercy Lord. I ask that you would cover this person in your precious blood. I ask for you to provide love, healing, comfort, peace, joy, strength, mercy, grace, compassion, deliverance, and many blessings to the person who is reading this. I believe all things are possible through you Jesus .I thank you in advance for answering this prayer Lord. I ask of these things in Jesus' name, Amen.

And whatever you ask in My name, that I will do, that the Father may be glorified in the Son. If you ask anything in My name, I will do it. John 14:13-14 New King James Version (NKJV)

# All things are possible

In conclusion, no matter what you are going through, your circumstances, or situations know that with God all things are possible! Don't allow anyone to tell you He can't do something. Obedience is better than sacrifice. Always listen to God! I have seen God do many things, but most of all He is who changed me to the woman I am today still on my journey with the Lord.

But He said, "The things which are impossible with men are possible with God." Luke 18:27 New King James Version (NKJV)

You are of God, little children, and have overcome them, because He who is in you is greater than he who is in the world. 1 John 4:4 New King James Version (NKJV)

# How to be born again

God wants every one of us to know Him personally and to become His child. The only way we can get to know God is through His son Jesus Christ. If you want you can ask from your heart.

In fact, it says,

"The message is very close at hand;
 it is on your lips and in your heart."

And that message is the very message about faith that we preach: If you openly declare that Jesus is Lord and believe in your heart that God raised him from the dead, you will be saved. For it is by believing in your heart that you are made right with God, and it is by openly declaring your faith that you are saved. Romans 10:8-10 New Living Translation (NLT)

## <u>You are more than</u>

You are more than your past and your failures, you are more than your look and those who are in magazines and books. You are of treasure that can't be measured. You are worth more than diamonds and gold. You are worth more than pearls, rubies, and gems that are sold. Haven't you been told? You must realize you are more than your hips and you thighs, your more than your hair and the make -up you apply. You are more than the scars that you hide. You are a child of God, the most high.

Madiline M Belle

# **Notes**

# Notes

_____

_____

_____

_____

_____

_____

_____

_____

_____

_____

_____

_____

_____

_____

_____

_____

_____

_____

www.ingramcontent.com/pod-product-compliance
Lightning Source LLC
Chambersburg PA
CBHW060121050426

42448CB00010B/1979